COMMON GARDEN BIRD CALLS

HANNU JÄNNES &
OWEN ROBERTS

NEW
HOLLAND

First published in 2009 by New Holland Publishers (UK) Ltd
London • Cape Town • Sydney • Auckland
www.newhollandpublishers.com

Garfield House, 86–88 Edgware Road, London W2 2EA, UK
80 McKenzie Street, Cape Town 8001, South Africa
Unit 1, 66 Gibbes Street, Chatswood, New South Wales, Australia 2067
218 Lake Road, Northcote, Auckland, New Zealand

1 3 5 7 9 10 8 6 4 2

ISBN 978 1 84773 517 1

Senior Editor: Krystyna Mayer
Designer: Peter Gwyer
Maps: Joseph Muise
Production: Melanie Dowland
Publisher: Simon Papps
Editorial Direction: Rosemary Wilkinson

Reproduction by Pica Digital (Pte) Ltd, Singapore
Printed and bound in Singapore by Craft Print International Ltd

CONTENTS

INSIDE BACK COVER –
CD WITH 60 BIRD CALLS

INTRODUCTION TO BIRD SOUNDS

Bird sounds – of one sort or another – are everywhere. These sounds can vary greatly: thrushes sing beautiful songs, woodpeckers drum on tree trunks and some birds click their wing feathers together or make snapping sounds with their beaks. This book and CD deal mainly with bird calls.

Most birds sing at dawn as soon as the sun rises; this is called the 'dawn chorus'. If you have never heard it, get up early and go out into your garden. Listen to how many different types of bird are calling at once and just how wonderful the sound is. Birds call early because sound travels best in the cool morning air, and this means that many more neighbours will hear their song.

There are as many different bird calls as there are different species of bird. Some birds, like the Blackbird and Robin, have beautiful songs, while others – the Carrion Crow and Grey Heron, for example – have harsh, unmusical voices.

Birds use their calls for many different reasons, but most often to protect their territory or to find a mate. Some birds, such as Meadow Pipits for instance, call from the tops of bushes or from fence posts. They do this either to tell others that the territory is taken, or to tell mates that they have a territory and are ready to raise chicks. Watch how Magpies chatter as they fight over your garden, each laying claim to the territory for raising its young.

During the winter Black-headed Gulls have a white head with just a dark spot behind the eye.

HOW TO USE THIS BOOK

- This book, together with the CD, will teach you to recognize some of the amazing sounds our birds make. The book features a photograph and some information on each of the 60 birds. It tells you where to find them, if they are here all year or if they are only visiting us, what they eat and how they nest. A map next to each bird shows where you can look for it.

- Use the CD with the book to match the pictures of the birds with the sounds they make. The track numbers on the CD correspond with the numbering of the birds in the book.
- As you learn and remember the sounds, you will be able to look for those birds when you hear them. Simply follow the call and look for the bird that's making it.

CD track number and common name of bird.

Map showing where in Britain and Ireland the bird can be seen.

KEY:
- ■ Resident
- ■ Winter
- ■ Summer
- □ Does not occur

Icons indicating food and nesting information.

Information about the call and the corresponding track number.

37 | Goldcrest

The Goldcrest has the distinction, with the much rarer Firecrest, of being Britain's smallest bird. Dull green above and whitish below, a bold white wing-bar and a splendid gold (yellow in the female) crown add distinction to its plumage. It moves constantly through the canopy, calling *si-si-si*, and outside the breeding season is often found in the company of tit flocks. It is mainly resident and found in most of Britain where there are woods, parks and gardens, but has a preference for conifers.

 Aphids and other small insects.

 Nest consists of a hammock of moss and lichens, which is usually hung beneath a conifer branch.

TRACK N° 37

Remarkably high-pitched, rhythmic song, *treddle-e-dee*, repeated often and ending in a flourish. Then equally high pitched *zee-zee*, *zee-zee* calls.

38 | Blue Tit

The Blue Tit is common in gardens, parks and woods throughout Britain. A tiny ball of blue and yellow with white cheeks, its acrobatics as it hangs upside down from branches and bird tables, to which it is a frequent visitor, are a source of much delight to the garden bird lover. It has small wings and a rather feeble, fluttering flight. In winter it is often found in reed beds, which provide it with both food and shelter. It is mainly resident in Britain.

 Aphids and small insects supplemented with seeds, nuts, fruits and fat from bird feeders.

 Nests in a lined hole in a tree, stump, post or wall.

TRACK N° 38

The song, including the short *tsee-tzi-tzii* and the beautiful high-pitched, silvery *biibi-sisisisi-srrrrrrr*. Then various calls including *churr* notes.

26

LEARNING ABOUT BIRDS FROM THEIR CALLS

Different birds have different calls. What's more, if you watch and listen closely, you will notice that the same bird makes a range of sounds. Each call serves a different purpose.

Young Blackbirds, for example, have one call to tell their parents where they are, and another to call for food. The first call encourages their parents to stay close by; the second makes the parents set off to fetch food for their young. Most birds have an alarm call to tell others that danger is near and that they should leave the area. 'Display' calls tell females that the male is looking for a mate.

Listening to bird calls is a good way of finding out what birds are up to, which opens up for us the amazing world of bird behaviour. After hearing a particular call, we can even start to predict what a bird will do next. Choose a bird in your garden and watch it closely. Write down each of its calls – as they sound to you – in a book, as well as what the bird was doing when it made that sound. If you do this regularly, you will soon start to understand the reasons why birds call and sing – in other words, to understand their language.

Please act responsibly when using the CD with this book. Birds can get upset when they hear other calls, and you may be interfering with breeding and even cause the birds to leave your area, thinking others are there already. If possible, do not play the calls in the wild at all. Rather listen at home, enjoy and learn. It is much better to listen to real birds in your garden than chase them away and be left with only a CD of bird calls.

Most importantly, listen and enjoy.

Male (left); female (right).

1 | Mallard

The Mallard is by far the most common and most frequently seen duck in Britain, resident wherever there is fresh water. Mallards often interbreed with 'farmyard' ducks so can be quite variable, but pure-bred birds are easy to identify.

The male has a conspicuous glossy green head and neck, a rusty-brown breast and a bright yellow bill. The female is quite different – a rather more drab variegated brown with a dark brown bill that has orangey edges. The feet are orange in both sexes.

A dabbling duck, the Mallard does not dive for food as some ducks do, but feeds by upending to immerse its head below the water's surface. It can be very tame, and those found around ponds in populated areas often take bread from the hand.

Mallards are found anywhere near fresh water – around ponds, ditches and streams. In gardens they may be seen where there are ponds or streams, or as they are flying overhead.

 Omnivorous. Mallards will eat almost anything – plant matter, worms, snails, insects and shellfish are all equally acceptable. Insects make up the bulk of the diet of ducklings. Birds that are used to humans will take bread, grain and cereal.

 Constructs a nest of grass and dead leaves lined with duck down in a wide range of nest sites, ranging from trees to flowerbeds near houses, but always in good ground cover near water. Between eight and twelve grey-green eggs are laid in February to October.

TRACK N° 01

Series of loud *quacks* by female. The much quieter calls of a feeding flock include lower pitched and softer calls by male, and a sharp *wiu*-whistle by male when guarding a female.

2 | Grey Heron

The only heron species that is common in Britain, the Grey Heron is resident throughout the year, occurring in almost any place where there is water or damp ground. A large grey, white and black bird measuring nearly a metre tall, it is most often seen standing by shallow water or in a wet field. In flight it looks huge, with its neck drawn in, hunched between its shoulders. It has taken to feeding at garden ponds, much to the dismay of owners of ornamental fish.

 Diet is mainly fish, frogs, newts and beetles, but as an opportunist it also takes small mammals and the young of ground-nesting birds.

 Nests colonially in branches of tall trees, building a huge, shallow platform of sticks.

 TRACK N° 02

Various harsh raucous flight calls based around a croaking *kark*.

3 | Common Buzzard

A large raptor with very broad wings, the Common Buzzard is basically dark brown with variable amounts of white on the underbody and wings. It has a heavy, slow flight, and when soaring it holds its wings in a shallow V. Common Buzzards have increased greatly in recent decades due to a reduction in persecution, and are now found in many wooded areas that have access to open country where they can hunt. In gardens they are most often seen and heard flying high overhead.

 Mainly small mammals, especially young rabbits, and carrion, frogs, worms and beetles.

 Builds a bulky stick nest in a tree, or more occasionally on a ledge on a crag or coastal cliff.

 TRACK N° 03

Quite vocal for a bird of prey, particularly in the breeding season. Mewing, plaintive calls are usually uttered in flight, but also while perched.

Female (left); male (right).

4 | Sparrowhawk

The second most common raptor after the Kestrel, the Sparrowhawk is resident in most wooded parts of Britain. It is a rather small bird of prey with a long tail and short, broad wings. Male and female birds differ markedly in plumage markings and size.

The brown-backed female is about 25 per cent larger than the grey-backed male. The male has blue-grey upper-parts, russet cheeks, finely barred orangey-red underparts, dark bars on the tail and dark wing tips. The upper-parts of the female are mainly dark brown, and she has white underparts with fine grey-brown horizontal bars, and a whitish tail with darker bars.

Although Sparrowhawks are typically birds of open countryside, woodland and hedgerows, they can often be seen dashing low across gardens and parks, having learned that bird feeders put out by humans can provide an easy meal.

The Sparrowhawk's long tail and short wings provide excellent manoeuvrability, allowing it to move at speed through wooded areas to snatch small birds like tits, finches and sparrows by surprise. Females can also take larger birds up to the size of Woodpigeons.

Builds a substantial platform of twigs in a broadleaf or conifer tree, often on the remains of an old crow's nest or squirrel's drey. The nest is built by the female, and between April and July three to six bluish-white eggs are laid. The male brings food to the brooding female at the nest.

TRACK N° 04

Only vocal near nest during breeding season, producing a quiet, chattering *keh-keh-keh-keh*. Recently fledged juveniles utter loud and demanding *kee-kee-kee-kee* begging calls.

5 | Kestrel

The Kestrel is Britain's most common bird of prey, and is the bird that can often be seen hanging in the air on quivering wings over motorway verges, which provide good hunting. Both sexes have rich warm brown backs and grey rumps and tails, and the male has a grey head. Kestrels are often seen perched on roadside wires and lamp posts, when they present a crouched, long-tailed outline. They are resident throughout Britain.

 Rodents, especially voles. Kestrels will also take insects, but rarely birds, probably lacking the speed with which to catch them. They may visit bird tables for meat scraps and fat.

 Nests on ledges of cliffs or buildings, and in tree holes and old crow's nests.

TRACK N° 05

Rapid series of sharp *kee-kee-kee-kee* notes, first uttered by male, followed by slightly coarser calls by female.

6 | Moorhen

Often confused by the beginner with the larger Coot, this is the blackish and slate-grey bird with a bright red, yellow-tipped bill and white on the under-tail. A mainly resident bird, it is common everywhere (except on high ground) where there are ponds, small lakes, waterside meadows, canals and slow-moving rivers and streams that have nearby dense vegetation. It swims with a series of jerky head and tail movements, and when feeding on land pecks and behaves like a hen.

 Aquatic plants, molluscs, insects, worms, seeds and grass.

 Builds a nest of reeds, grass and sedges almost always just out of the water.

TRACK N° 06

The Moorhen is more often heard than seen. Its various calls include a nasal *prrruwkk* and sharp, rubber toy-like *kwe-ick*.

7 | Pheasant

Native to eastern Asia, the Pheasant was introduced to Britain by humans and was first mentioned in the literature in 1059. The male is unmistakable, with his green head, the bare red skin on his face and his very long tail. The female is a more subdued brown with dark spots. Resident in open woodland, farmland with dense cover and large gardens in rural areas, Pheasants are most common where they are artificially reared for the shoot. When disturbed they rise with a clatter and whirring wings.

 Seeds, fruits, berries, roots and insects.

 Nests in ground cover, in a hollow sparsely lined with grass and leaves.

8 | Black-headed Gull

By far the most common and widespread of Britain's small gulls, the name of the Black-headed Gull is a misnomer: its head is actually chocolate-brown, and then only in the breeding season, with the dark colour decreasing to a mere ear spot in winter. It is not confined to the seashore and may be abundant inland near water, where it will readily come to take bread. In gardens it is mostly seen flying overhead, but may sometimes visit in noisy gangs in winter.

 Can often be seen following the plough to feed on worms and insects that have been disturbed, but will also eat grain, scraps and invertebrates.

 Nests colonially, sometimes in large numbers, in tussocks or flat ground by lakes, ponds and coastal marshes.

TRACK N° 07
Display call of male is a loud, far-carrying *karck-kah*, normally followed by a quick audible whirr of wings. Another call (not on CD) is a loud *kh'kh'kh...*, uttered by both sexes.

TRACK N° 08
Very vocal, particularly at breeding colonies and feeding sites. Slurred, screeching calls, initially by a single individual, then the cacophony of a breeding colony.

9 | Stock Dove

Although the Stock Dove is found throughout Britain apart from the west and north of Scotland, it only usually occurs in rural habitats, and in town parks and gardens with mature trees. It lacks the white on the wing and neck of the Woodpigeon, and has a flitting rather than a powerful wing action in flight. The Stock Dove is similar to some feral pigeons, but is rarely found in their preferred habitats (see right).

 Grains, weeds (especially charlock), young shoots and seedlings.

 Nests in holes in trees, ruined farm buildings and even old rabbit burrows.

10 | Feral Pigeon

This feral descendant of the now rare Rock Dove is the common pigeon of Britain's town and city streets, and parks and gardens. Some individuals remain true to their ancestral form and are pale grey with black wing bars and a white rump, but interbreeding with lost homing pigeons has resulted in a wide variety of plumage colours, including a considerable amount of white, brown or even black.

 Grain, seeds and other morsels, especially bread fed to it by humans.

 Wild Rock Doves nest on rocky coasts and mountain cliffs. Feral pigeons replicate this habitat, using ledges on buildings and in ruins for their nests.

TRACK N° 09

A deep two-note advertising call, *ooo-wuhh-ooo-wuh*, which is repeated 8–9 times in a series.

TRACK N° 10

Various cooing sounds that are very deep and hollow sounding, and not very far carrying in the noisy environment in which they live.

11 | Woodpigeon

Found throughout Britain wherever there are trees or large bushes to roost in and nest in, this is a bulky pigeon that has white patches on its neck and wings. It is the bird that can surprise you in wooded areas when it takes off with a loud clatter of wings. Woodpigeons are often seen in display flight climbing rapidly to a height, clapping their wings, then gliding slowly downwards. They are resident in Britain and augmented in the winter with many more individuals from northern and eastern continental Europe.

 Seeds, clover, peas and cereals throughout the year, plus beech mast and acorns in autumn.

 A flimsy platform of twigs, which is easily seen from below, is built in a tree, bush or large hedge.

TRACK N° 11

The commonly heard song or advertising call is a deep, five-syllable hooting, with a very characteristic rhythm.

12 | Collared Dove

Unknown in Britain until the 1950s, the Collared Dove spread rapidly across Europe from Asia in the 1900s, and is now common and widespread. It particularly favours parks and gardens in towns, and farms and villages in rural areas. It is a small, slim dove with pale buff plumage that is relieved only by black wing tips and the black collar from which it takes its name. It often perches on roadside wires, roofs and chimneys.

 Seeds and grain. The species' rapid expansion across Europe has been attributed to its exploitation of sources of spilt grain. It often visits garden feeders.

 Builds a platform nest in a dense tree, usually a conifer, near farms, in town parks and gardens, and in villages.

TRACK N° 12

The commonly heard advertising call is a repeated trisyllabic hollow cooing with a characteristic rhythm. A thin nasal *eerrrr* (not on CD) is given in flight and in excitement.

13 | Tawny Owl

With its hooting call, the Tawny Owl is more often heard than seen. It occurs widely (except in Ireland) where there are large, mature trees, including in large suburban gardens. Strictly nocturnal, it is most often seen in the headlights of vehicles. More rarely it is chanced upon at a daytime roost in a tree hole or pressed close against the trunk of a tree, its presence often betrayed by the small birds that can be seen mobbing it.

 Small mammals, especially mice, provide the bulk of the Tawny Owl's diet, but it will also take small birds and insects, and sometimes young rabbits and squirrels.

 Usually nests in a hollow tree, but also in rocks, old crow's nests and even rabbit holes.

TRACK N° 13
Song is a series of hollow-sounding hooting notes: a strong hoot, a pause, a short hoot, then a shivering sequence of rapid *hoo-ing*. Contact call is a loud, sharp *ke-vick*.

14 | Green Woodpecker

This striking woodpecker that is nearly as big as a Jackdaw is green with a red crown and a yellow rump. It has an unmistakable bounding flight, closing its wings after every few beats, and to top it all a unique manic call. It climbs trees in jerky hops, but unlike most European woodpeckers also feeds readily on the ground. It rarely drums, and does so only softly despite its powerful bill. Green Woodpeckers are resident and widely but thinly distributed in Britain in areas with scattered mature trees.

 Wood-boring larvae in trees, while on the ground the long, sticky tongue is adept at sweeping up ants. In winter it also takes berries, nuts and acorns.

 Excavates a relatively large hole in a tree.

TRACK N° 14
First two sets of 'yaffling' *hwahwahwahwa* calls, followed by two sets of chuckling flight calls.

15 | Great Spotted Woodpecker

A predominantly black and white woodpecker, the male has a red crown, and both sexes have red under-tails. Two pied woodpeckers are found in Britain, but this is the largest and by far the most likely to be seen, being common in woodland, parks and gardens even on the urban fringe. Its loud, rapid drumming is a commonly heard sound of the countryside, and is made by banging the bill against dead trees, telegraph poles and even metal objects. It rarely visits the ground, but is a frequent visitor at bird tables.

 Wood-boring larvae, insects, the nestlings of other birds and in winter conifer seeds.

 Excavates a hole in a tree that is much smaller than that of the Green Woodpecker.

TRACK N° 15

First drumming (made by both sexes), which is short and fades towards the end. Then the *kick* call heard throughout the year.

16 | Skylark

Everyone knows the Skylark because of its song, but to look at it is a rather nondescript greyish-brown bird with darker streaks and a whitish belly. Other than its song, the often raised crest on its crown is its most conspicuous feature. Skylarks are resident in Britain, and the population is augmented with many birds that come to winter from the north. They are frequently common on farmland, heaths, meadows, moors, coastal marshes and dunes, and form flocks in winter on stubble and ploughed land. In gardens they are mostly seen flying overhead.

 Insects, weeds and seeds.

 Builds a simple cup of dried grass in grassland or crops, often in the hoof print of a cow or horse.

TRACK N° 16

First the song, which consists of a lengthy outpouring of chirrups and whistles given at height, then *pruit* flight calls.

17 | Common Swift

The only swift species commonly occurring in Britain, the Common Swift is a summer visitor from southern Africa, spending only a very short time here from late April/early May to early September. An unmistakable bird with a short, forked tail and long, scythe-shaped wings, it appears all black at a distance. It is perfectly adapted to life in the air and rarely lands other than at the nest, even sleeping on the wing. Small parties are frequently seen on still summer evenings as they 'scream' through towns and villages.

 Exclusively insects caught on the wing.

 Nests colonially, usually in association with humans, beneath roof tiles, and in holes in eaves and church towers.

 TRACK N° 17

First shrill, screaming flight calls, then (similar) calls from birds roosting at their nest holes.

18 | Swallow

The Swallow is a common sight in the countryside, particularly around farms and villages. Its plumage consists of blue-black upper-parts, pale and pale buff underparts relieved only by a bright chestnut chin, and long tail streamers. A summer visitor from southern Africa, it arrives in April and leaves in September, when it is a common if somewhat melancholic sight lined up on telegraph wires prior to departure, heralding the end of summer.

 Feeds almost exclusively on insects taken on the wing.

 Swallows originally built a cup of mud in a cave or on rocks, but have evolved a close association with humans and now erect their nests in outbuildings, porches and sheds instead.

 TRACK N° 18

A melodious twittering and sputtering song, interspersed with a strangled croak, followed by a trilling rattle. Females use the length of the rattle to evaluate the fitness of the males.

19 | House Martin

The House Martin is a summer visitor from tropical Africa from April to September/October. Although it is similar to the Swallow in being blue-black above and white below, it presents a more compact shape and has no tail streamers, but a very visible white rump. It frequents towns, villages and farms – anywhere there is a nearby supply of soft mud to build a nest with and something to build it on. It is found in most of Britain.

 Insects taken on the wing, but usually at a much higher level than those taken by the Swallow.

 Nests colonially, building a cup of mud that is attached to a building, bridge or cliff. Lines of these mud cups under eaves are a common sight in rural Britain.

TRACK N° 19

Short, dry stony rattles by birds visiting their nests.

20 | Meadow Pipit

This rather unremarkable small bird is olive-brown streaked darker above, and whitish-buff below with black streaks. Its legs are noticeably pinkish. It is common throughout Britain in open country, especially on heaths and moors, and in coastal grasslands and salting. It forms small flocks in winter on open farmland, in marshy areas and around the coast. Spring and autumn migrants fly over all habitats. During its spring display it flies up from the ground, sometimes to quite a height, before 'parachuting' back to the ground, singing throughout. In gardens it is mostly seen flying overhead.

 Insects, small worms and some seeds.

 Constructs a neat, closely woven cup of grass well hidden in heather, rough grass, rushes or tussocks.

TRACK N° 20

Song of a 'parachuting' bird repeats the *tsiltsilptsilptsliptsilp* theme, and *ist istt* calls are usually given on taking flight.

21 | Grey Wagtail

This is a typical wagtail, being quite small, but with a proportionately long tail that is constantly in motion. A rather striking bird, it is grey above and white below, with bright yellow on the breast and under-tail. It is fairly common where there are fast-flowing rivers and streams with exposed rocks for perches. Although it is mainly resident, in winter it often moves to lower ground around lakes, slow-flowing rivers and estuaries.

 Mainly insects and small crustaceans.

 Builds a nest of rootlets and grass in a rock crevice, bank, bridge or building, always close to running water.

22 | Pied Wagtail

A small black and white bird with a long, frequently 'wagged' tail, the Pied Wagtail is a familiar sight throughout Britain, even in the hearts of cities. It is resident and found only in Britain and the near Continent, and is replaced by its close relative, the White Wagtail, in the remainder of Europe. Outside the breeding season it roosts gregariously – dozens, even hundreds, of birds can often be seen going to roost in trees and on buildings in towns and cities.

 Insects that are caught by running on the ground.

 Forms a nest of grass and roots, usually in a recess in a wall or building.

TRACK N° 21

High-pitched song and low-frequency calls – typical for birds living near noisy rivers. First a tinkling series of song strophes of varying phrases of notes, then a series of rapid calls.

TRACK N° 22

First the slowly advancing (with long pauses) song of *tsitsellittt* notes, then some disyllabic *tsli-vitt* calls, often given when taking flight.

23 | Wren

The tiny Wren with its stumpy cocked tail and incongruously loud song is one of Britain's most familiar birds. It is a resident, and can suffer badly during hard winters. It is found almost everywhere, from inner city gardens to remote Scottish islands, and feeds low in vegetation and in nooks and crannies in walls or cliffs, where it is unobtrusive and more often heard than seen. Normally fiercely territorial in winter, it will roost communally, with up to 20 birds crammed together in a suitable cavity.

 Small insects and spiders, with seeds added in winter.

 Builds a dome of grass, leaves and lichens in a hedge, ivy, wall or shed. Males build 'cock nests' for apparently no reason, as they are never used.

TRACK N° 23

An amazingly loud song with trills, then rattling hard *zerrrrr* calls and sharp, clicking call notes.

24 | Dunnock

A sparrow-sized bird that is often described as drab, close inspection reveals that the Dunnock's brown-streaked upper-parts, set against a lavender-grey head, breast and belly, are really quite attractive in a quiet sort of way. Resident in Britain, it is common in both town gardens and parks, and in open woodlands and hedges on farmland in rural areas. Other than in late winter and spring, when it proclaims its territory by singing from a pen perch, it is unobtrusive, feeding in leaf litter below trees and hedges.

 Insects and other small invertebrates, and seeds.

 Constructs a foundation of twigs on which a cup of grass and moss is built in a hedge or bush.

TRACK N° 24

First a short song, which is often given from the top of a bush, hedge or wall around a garden, then the *tliihi* flight call.

25 | Robin

Probably Britain's favourite, and certainly best-known bird, the Robin is a plump and upright bird with a red breast that is actually more orange than red. It is a familiar year-round sight in parks, gardens and woodlands. Well known for pugnacity with their own kind and for being fearless of humans, Robins will take worms from the hand and are rarely shy, becoming skulking only when nesting. They are resident throughout Britain, and the population is swelled in winter with arrivals from colder parts of Europe.

 Ground-dwelling insects and worms, supplemented by berries, seeds and soft fruits in autumn and winter.

 Builds a bulky nest for its size, from moss, grass and dead leaves, in a hole in a wall, shed or tree.

TRACK N° 25

First the song, heard most of the year except in the post-breeding season. It is more eager in spring, but somewhat melancholic/wistful in autumn and winter. Then ticking call notes.

26 | Song Thrush

A familiar bird of woodland, parks and gardens throughout Britain, the Song Thrush is resident, with more individuals arriving in autumn from the Continent to take advantage of the milder winters. It is the brown-backed bird with a spotted breast and belly seen feeding on lawns in gardens and parks, pulling worms from the ground. It begins to sing as early as December.

 Worms, snails and insects, with seeds and berries in winter. Often uses a stone in the ground as an 'anvil' on which to smash snail shells in order to extract the snails inside.

 Constructs a finely woven cup of moss and grass lined with mud in a tree, bush or shed, often in gardens.

 TRACK N° 26

A loud song to advertise its often hidden presence in tree branches, then sharp, thin *tick* calls, and finally a chattering warning call near the nest.

27 | Mistle Thrush

A larger, more robust version of the Song Thrush, the Mistle Thrush is paler overall, especially on the back, which is greyish-brown. It has a markedly undulating flight like that of a woodpecker. It sings loudly from tree tops, often in poor weather, giving it the country name of 'Storm-cock'. Mainly resident in parks, gardens and woodlands (including those with conifers) throughout Britain, it can also be found in open fields and on low moors in winter.

 Worms, snails and insects, and also ripe berries, especially in autumn, when it visits the hills for rowan and juniper berries.

 Builds a cup of grass, moss and roots lined with mud and wool at varying heights in the fork of a tree.

TRACK N° 27
First the song, which is clear, loud and insistent, given from an exposed perch in a tree top, then a dry rattling call.

28 | Redwing

The Redwing is a winter visitor to Britain, with large numbers sometimes arriving from Scandinavia in late September/October, and leaving in March/early April. It is similar to the Song Thrush, but has rusty-red flanks and under-wings, and a bright whitish stripe above the eye. It can be seen in flocks, often with Fieldfares and Song Thrushes, in fields or in open woods, gardens and parks where there are berry bushes. Listen for calling migrants, especially at night.

 Worms and insects in fields, but equally fond of berries, especially those of holly, ivy and yew.

 The Redwing nests only occasionally in Britain.

TRACK N° 28
Two examples of the variable song, then the *chuk–chuk* warning call, and finally the *srii* flight call.

29 | Fieldfare

A winter visitor from Scandinavia present in Britain from October to March, the Fieldfare is of robust build, like the Mistle Thrush, but has a grey head and rump, and the spots on its chest and belly are shaped like arrowheads. It utters a very loud *chakk* call when disturbed. Highly gregarious when in Britain, it feeds with other thrushes on insect-rich fields and berry-laden trees and bushes. In gardens calling birds are mostly heard as they fly overhead, but Fieldfares can be attracted to gardens by windfall apples.

 Worms, insects, berries and fallen apples.

 The Fieldfare rarely nests in Britain.

TRACK N° 29

Song not included because it is a winter visitor to the UK. Calls include a variable low cackling and *chakk* notes repeated several times in succession.

30 | Blackbird

The Blackbird is familiar throughout Britain in gardens, parks, hedgerows and woodlands. The male is unmistakable, being black all over with a bright orange-yellow bill, but his mate is a more subdued dark brown with a paler throat and breast and a blackish-brown bill. When disturbed the Blackbird gives a loud, scolding *chink-chink* call as it disappears into cover. It has a beautiful song and a limited song period from February through July.

 Worms, insects, snails, berries, soft fruits and fallen apples.

 Constructs a large, cup-shaped nest of grass, moss and leaves lined with mud in a hedge, bush or small tree, or occasionally in a wall or shed or in ground cover.

TRACK N° 30

The stunningly beautiful fluty song, then the *srii* call, and finally the loud, hysterical *chink–chink–chink*.

31 | Sedge Warbler

The Sedge Warbler is small, brown above and streaked darker, with unmarked buff-white underparts. Two things attract attention in this bird – the bold, creamy stripe above the eye, and the oft-repeated song flight as it rises vertically from the vegetation with a harsh chattering, before quickly dropping back to cover again. A summer visitor from April to September, the Sedge Warbler is common where there is thick vegetation close to water, and has a preference for small ponds, ditches and marshy areas. It may be seen in gardens that adjoin wetlands.

 Gnats, midges, aquatic insects and small molluscs.

 A neat, shallow cup of grass and moss is constructed in low herbage, rarely more than a metre from the ground.

 TRACK N° 31

The flight song, followed by the *teck* calls.

32 | Common Whitethroat

This is a small, slim warbler with a longish tail. The male has a grey head, white throat and rust-coloured wings. The female lacks the grey head. The species is a common summer visitor from Africa, remaining in Britain from April to September. It is abundant in areas of scrub, coastal heath and farmland with good hedge cover, and can usually be seen briefly during its low, jerky song flight above a hedge or scrub, before it dives into deep cover. It can sometimes be very skulking, but at other times will sing happily from an open situation. It prefers rural gardens with bushes.

 Mainly insects, but also berries and fruits.

 A cup of grass is built close to the ground in dense herbage, brambles, thick hedgerows or bushes.

 TRACK N° 32

The flight song, followed by nervous, nasal *dverh-dverh-dverh* calls.

23

33 | Garden Warbler

This very nondescript, unobtrusive warbler is greyish-brown above, paler below. It is found throughout Britain (except the far north and west) where there are woods with clearings and parks and gardens that have large trees and good ground cover. It is a summer visitor from tropical Africa, arriving in late April and gone from British shores by late September. Often difficult to see due to its preference for dense cover, it is best detected by its song – loud and given from low down in a dense bush or herbage.

 Mainly insects, and some soft fruits and berries in late summer and early autumn.

 Builds a cup of grass and hair low down in dense bushes, brambles or herbage.

TRACK N° 33

The song is a beautiful warble lasting a few seconds, not unlike that of the Blackcap, but almost always delivered from low, dense cover. The call is an irritable *chek-chek*.

34 | Blackcap

Blackcaps are mainly summer visitors to Britain from North Africa and the western Mediterranean, but increasing numbers now winter here around gardens, where they can regularly be seen at bird tables. The male is grey above with a black cap, the female brown above with a rusty-red cap. Blackcaps are found wherever there is broadleaved or mixed woodland, even in large gardens in urban areas. Their loud, rich warbling song attracts the attention, but the birds are often difficult to see in the leafy canopy.

 Insects supplemented with soft fruits and berries in autumn and winter.

 Makes a tightly woven cup of grass and sedges in brambles, thick bushes or ivy.

TRACK N° 34

The rich, warbling song, followed by the *tack* call.

35 | Chiffchaff

This nondescript, small grey-green bird is often described as drab or dingy. Its oft-repeated *chiff-chaff* song is as unremarkable as its appearance, but it is a commonly heard sound in the spring and autumn countryside, wherever the favoured habitat of open, preferably tall trees with an understorey is present. Although Chiffchaffs were formerly only summer visitor to Britain, increasing numbers now spend milder winters with us.

 Aphids, small larvae and spiders are picked from leaves. Chiffchaffs often sally from trees or bushes to catch flying insects.

 Builds a domed nest of grass, dead leaves and moss in herbage, brambles or small bushes.

TRACK N° 35

The repetitive *chiff-chaff, chiff-chaff* song, followed by the *hyit* call.

36 | Willow Warbler

The Willow Warbler is a small, inconspicuous bird, very like the Chiffchaff, but a brighter greenish-grey above and a cleaner white below, with a more noticeable whitish stripe through the eye and pale rather than dark legs. It is well known for its beautiful song, a descending series of soft whistles, which it sings after its arrival from Africa in April. It leaves in late August to October. Willow Warblers are very common where there are trees and bushes, from upland birches down to large lowland gardens.

 Almost exclusively insects, particularly aphids picked from leaves, and small caterpillars.

 A domed nest of grass is constructed on or in close proximity to the ground, in good cover.

TRACK N° 36

The song followed by the *hyy-it* call, which is very similar to the call of a Chiffchaff, but slightly more up-slurred at the end.

37 | Goldcrest

The Goldcrest has the distinction, with the much rarer Firecrest, of being Britain's smallest bird. Dull green above and whitish below, a bold white wing-bar and a splendid gold (yellow in the female) crown add distinction to its plumage. It moves constantly through the canopy, calling *zee-zee*, and outside the breeding season is often found in the company of tit flocks. It is mainly resident and found in most of Britain where there are woods, parks and gardens, but has a preference for conifers.

 Aphids and other small insects.

 Nest consists of a hammock of moss and lichens, which is usually hung beneath a conifer branch.

TRACK N° 37

Remarkably high-pitched, rhythmic song, *treddle-e-dee*, repeated often and ending in a flourish. Then equally high pitched *zee-zee, zee-zee* calls.

38 | Blue Tit

The Blue Tit is common in gardens, parks and woods throughout Britain. A tiny ball of blue and yellow with white cheeks, its acrobatics as it hangs upside down from branches and bird tables, to which it is a frequent visitor, are a source of much delight to the garden bird lover. It has small wings and a rather feeble, fluttering flight. In winter it is often found in reed beds, which provide it with both food and shelter. It is mainly resident in Britain.

 Aphids and small insects supplemented with seeds, nuts, fruits and fat from bird feeders.

 Nests in a lined hole in a tree, stump, post or wall.

TRACK N° 38

The song, including the short *tsee-tzi-tzii* and the beautiful high-pitched, silvery *biibi-sisisisi-srrrrrrr*. Then various calls including *churr* notes.

39 | Great Tit

Our largest tit, this species is mainly sedentary and is found commonly throughout Britain in woodland and garden habitats. It can be easily identified by its yellow underparts bisected with a black band, and its black head with white cheeks. Almost as acrobatic as its smaller cousin, the Blue Tit, it is a frequent visitor to bird tables, where it is bold and aggressive. Birdwatchers reckon that if you hear a bird call and do not know what it is, if you say it is a Great Tit you will probably be correct, because it has a bewildering variety of calls.

 Insects, small snails, worms, seeds, fruits, nuts and fat at feeders.

 Nests in a tree hole in almost any cavity, which it fills with grass, leaves and moss, and lines with hair.

TRACK N° 39

The simple song, varying a lot around the theme of *tee-ta, tee-ta, tee-ta*. Then three clear syllabic *twet-twet-twe* calls, and various scolding and purring calls.

40 | Coal Tit

This is Britain's smallest tit, and it is even marginally smaller than the Blue Tit. Resident throughout much of Britain, it is more closely associated with conifers than the other common tit species, and is often found in association with the Goldcrest. However, it does frequent mixed woods, parks and large gardens with conifers, and readily visits feeders. It is an attractive bird with a greyish back, buff underparts, two white wing-bars, and a black head with white cheeks and nape.

 Insects, seeds and nuts.

 Nests in a lined hole in a rotting tree stump, or in a hole in the ground among tree roots.

TRACK N° 40

Song a faster, far higher pitched version of the song of the Great Tit. Then some nasal *ty-ii* calls.

41 | Marsh Tit

This small tit is greyish-brown above and buff-white below, with a black cap and bib and white cheeks. It is sedentary, and is absent from Scotland and Ireland, and much of northern and western England. Despite its name it does not frequent marshes, but inhabits damp deciduous woods and copses that have not been thinned and have plenty of rotten timber. It favours gardens adjoining woodland, and often attracts attention by its explosive *pssi chew* call.

 Insects, seeds and berries, and visits bird feeders.

 Nests in a hole in a rotten tree trunk or stump, which it usually enlarges and lines with wool, hair and moss.

TRACK N° 41

Variable song – here a series of *twetwetwe...* repeated every three seconds. Diagnostic call is *shar pssi* or *pssi chew*, often with a scolding nasal *jhe jhe jhe jhe*.

42 | Long-tailed Tit

The Long-tailed Tit is basically black above and whitish below, with a white crown and a pinkish hue on the wings and flanks, and it is its shape – a tiny ball of fluffy feathers with an oversized tail and a minute bill – that lays claim to it being Britain's cutest bird. It usually travels in small groups, constantly calling zee-zee-zee, and although it is a weak flyer it is extremely acrobatic in the canopy. It occurs in deciduous and mixed woods, hedgerows, parks with bushes and large gardens throughout the British Isles, where it is mainly resident.

 Small insects and spiders, and seeds and fat at bird tables.

 Builds a beautifully constructed oval dome of wool, moss and lichens in a hedge or bush.

TRACK N° 42

First a series of dry, slurred *trrr* call notes and a single, drawn-out, high-pitched silvery trill, then some quiet *pt* notes, and finally the frequent high-pitched *zee-zee-zee* note.

43 | Nuthatch

The Nuthatch is the only British bird that can descend a tree head first.

An attractive woodpecker-like bird that is steel blue-grey above, rusty-buff below, and has a distinctive black eye-stripe and a relatively long, sharply pointed bill, the Nuthatch announces its presence in the tree canopy with loud, ringing calls. It is resident and common in much of England where there are deciduous or mixed woods, open parkland and large gardens adjoining woodland, but is absent from Scotland and Ireland.

The Nuthatch has the unique ability among Britain's birds to be able to run up or down tree trunks and larger branches in search of food. It extracts stored food, such as nuts in tree crevices, with several hefty blows of its powerful bill, making a tapping noise that may be heard for several hundred metres. The loud smashing noise sometimes resembles the drumming of a woodpecker.

An extremely active bird, the Nuthatch shows great agility as it climbs along branches in different directions, including downwards. It can also be seen on the ground, employing distinctive jerky hops as it feeds.

Mainly spiders and insects, including beetles and grubs in summer. More nuts and larger seeds are eaten in autumn, with hazelnuts, beechnuts and acorns being wedged into bark to be consumed later. In winter it visits bird tables, where it will take peanuts (which are also stored), seeds and fat.

Nuthatches line a hole in a tree trunk or wall with leaves, grass and bark. If the hole is too large it will be blocked with mud until the required size is achieved. They lay six to nine red-speckled white eggs between late April and June, and both parents feed the young.

TRACK N° 43

Two different song types, a rapid liquid trilling, *ve've've've've*, then a slow disyllabic *wee–wee* repeated every few seconds or so. Calls include an often repeated *tuiep*.

44 | Treecreeper

The Treecreeper does exactly what its name suggests, creeping mouse-like up and along, but never down, tree trunks and branches. Once finished with one tree it flies down to begin a spiral up another nearby. Like no other British bird, it is a mixture of browns and buffs above and whitish below, and has a very small body with a comparatively long, thin down-curved bill and a long, spiked tail that it presses against a tree for support. It is resident in Britain and found almost everywhere in wooded country. In winter it often roams with tit flocks.

 Almost exclusively small insects, but also occasionally seeds.

 The nest is built on a supporting platform of small twigs behind the loose bark of a tree or in ivy.

TRACK N° 44

A quiet but distinctive *swee-swee-swee* song followed by a trill, then the *tsree* call, and finally a very thin, high-pitched *tih* call.

45 | Magpie

An unmistakable large black and white crow with a very long tail, the Magpie is a common resident everywhere with the exception of the far north of Scotland. It occurs in a wide variety of habitats, usually near humans, because it has learned to recognize us as a source of easy food pickings and protection from predators.

 Will eat almost anything – carrion, scraps, nestlings, worms, insects, fruits and seeds.

 Constructs a huge domed nest of sticks that is very visible in a tree or large bush when leaf cover is absent.

TRACK N° 45

Magpies have a range of calls. The CD includes first a staccato chattering, then sharp *ch'chack* calls.

46 | Jay

The Jay is a member of the crow family and is one of the most striking of British birds. Pinkish-brown with blue and white in the wings, a white rump and throat, a black moustache, and a streaked black and white erectile crown, its colouration is quite different from that of the usual black of other crows. It is resident, but common only where there is good woodland cover, and can be seen in parks and large gardens. Jays are partial to acorns, which they hoard for winter in the autumn, and favour oak woods.

 Omnivorous, but frequently feeds on acorns, nuts and beech mast, and is a persistent thief of the eggs and nestlings of other birds.

 Erects a well-hidden, untidy platform of twigs and roots in a tree or bush.

TRACK N° 46

A variety of calls – here first strange conversational clucking notes, then a *chewchewchewchew...* series, and finally some common harsh and raucous calls.

47 | Jackdaw

This small, compact black crow can be recognized by its grey nape and pale eye. It is very gregarious and is often seen in wheeling flocks, especially in the evenings before it goes to roost communally. It is resident in Britain, and common everywhere with the exception of the far north of Scotland, inhabiting farmland, parks, towns, ruins and coastal cliffs.

 Mainly insects and worms, but also eggs and nestlings in spring, and fruits and corn in autumn.

 Nests colonially in cracks and holes in woods, on cliff faces, and in ruins and chimneys.

 TRACK N° 47

Typical *tjakk, khakk* or *kyak* calls, first from a group of birds near a breeding colony, then from a single individual.

48 | Rook

The adults of this glossy black crow can be distinguished from the similar Carrion Crow by the extensive area of greyish-white bare skin above the bill, and by the loose feathering around the thighs that gives them a 'baggy-trousered' look. The Rook is resident everywhere other than the central highlands of Scotland, and has a close association with humans. It nests colonially in isolated patches of trees, often in churchyards, on farmland, and around villages and rural towns, where its loud *caw* draws attention. When feeding on the ground it has a waddling gait like that of a duck.

 Insects, worms and some vegetable matter, especially corn.

 Nests colonially in a rookery, in a large and very obvious stick nest.

TRACK N° 48

Harsh and hoarse *graah* calls by a couple of individuals, then a near-deafening cacophony of sound from a rookery.

49 | Carrion Crow

The Carrion Crow is about the size of a Rook, but black all over without any particular distinguishing mark, and is more solitary in behaviour. It is resident throughout England, Wales and southern Scotland, and is replaced in the north of Scotland and in Ireland by the closely related Hooded Crow, a more striking black and grey bird. Catholic in choice of habitat, it is found in towns, on farmland, in woods, on moors and around sea cliffs, and visits bird tables in gardens.

 Will take almost anything – insects, small mammals and vegetable matter – but as its name suggests seems to have a particular liking for carrion.

 Builds a bulky, scruffy platform of sticks in a tree or large bush, or on a ledge.

TRACK N° 49

Very vocal, commonly heard call being *kraah* with some variation.

50 | House Sparrow

As its name suggests, this is a bird of built-up areas that has become very much tied to humans, to the extent that we have become the limiting factor in its distribution. It is brown streaked darker above and greyish-white below, and often looks rather scruffy, but the male does have a smart black bib and a grey crown. House Sparrows are resident and found everywhere where humans build their homes and factories, although they have recently declined in some parts of Britain.

 Seeds, insects and household scraps, especially bread.

 Often nests colonially under roof tiles, in gutters, on ledges on buildings, or more rarely in trees or bushes.

TRACK N° 50

The song is frequently interpreted as *chirp-chirp*, but is in fact *tselp-tselp*.

51 | Starling

Starlings are resident throughout Britain, but in winter there is a big immigration from colder climes to the north and east. It is then that the spectacle of huge flocks of birds can be observed in aerial display before going to roost in trees and reed beds, and on city buildings. Basically black with a yellow bill, in summer the Starling's plumage has a glossy green or purple sheen. In autumn and winter it is covered in whitish spots. It inhabits urban areas and is a common bird around town gardens, as well as in woods and around coastal cliffs. It is very sociable in all seasons.

 Insects and worms supplemented by seeds, soft fruits and cereals.

 Nests in holes, usually in walls or buildings, but also in trees and cliffs.

TRACK N° 51

First the song, which is a rich, rambling collection of rather strangled sounds, throaty warblings and musical whistles, including much mimicry. Then *thceerr* calls from a flock.

52 | Bullfinch

This large, plump finch with a stubby bill, the male with a bluish-grey back, reddish-pink underparts, black cap and white rump, is undoubtedly one of Britain's most attractive birds. The female is similarly patterned, but in more subdued hues. The Bullfinch has a retiring nature and is most frequently seen as a white rump fast disappearing into a hedgerow or bush. It is found everywhere except the far north, in scrub, rural gardens with Blackthorn or fruit trees, orchards and forest edges.

 Seeds, some insects and the buds of trees.

 Constructs an intricate platform of woven sticks in hedgerows, bushes or brambles.

TRACK N° 52

The male's song (which is not often heard) is a rambling twittering without clear phrases. The call is a piping single note given singly or in a series of 2–3 notes.

53 | Chaffinch

Mainly resident, the Chaffinch is Britain's most common finch, found everywhere there are open woods, hedges, parks and gardens. In winter, when numbers increase with visitors from further north, it frequents farmland, often in the company of other finches and sparrows. The male is a handsome bird sporting rusty-red cheeks and breast, and a blue-grey crown and neck. The female is a rather drab brown, but has a prominent white bar on the wing and a greenish rump that is visible when she is taking flight.

 Seeds and grain, with insects in spring and summer.

 Builds a superbly woven cup of moss, lichens and other available soft materials in a hedge or bush.

 TRACK N° 53

The cheerful song, then a *twink* (*pink, fink*) call, and an upwards inflected clear *hwet*.

54 | Greenfinch

This is a sturdy green finch with a heavy bill, a yellow wing-panel, and yellow sides to the tail that are conspicuous in flight. It is resident everywhere in relatively open habitat with some trees and bushes, and is thus common in gardens and parks even in built-up areas, as well as in open woodland and on farmland with hedgerows. It often perches on the tops of trees and bushes, attracting attention with a persistent nasal call.

 Seeds and berries, but feeds its young on insects. Attracted to bird tables by hemp and sunflower seeds.

 Builds a loose structure of twigs and grass lined with moss in a bush, tree or overgrown hedge.

TRACK N° 54

Two song types, the first a nasal, downwards inflected *djeeeeuuoo* (*sruuuoooo*) with pauses. Then a more complex song with slower notes – *djuw djuw djuw, jup jup jup, chi'di'di'di'di.*

55 | Goldfinch

This is a most attractive bird that was once much prized by the cage-bird trade. The sexes are alike, with stunning red, black and white heads and ivory-coloured bills. Some birds are resident, but many move south to France and Spain for the winter. Goldfinches are found everywhere (except parts of northern Scotland) where there are parks, large gardens, orchards and areas of scrub close to woodland edges.

 A specialized bill enables the Goldfinch to extract seeds from thistles and teasels, its main food source. It is common at bird tables that provide seeds.

 A neat cup of roots filled with moss, lichens and thistledown is constructed in a tree, large bush or dense hedge.

TRACK N° 55

A vocal bird with a variety of calls, here a bright, fast, tinkling rattling and trilling song, which is quite complex and usually recognizable by the inclusion of call notes.

56 | Siskin

A small green and yellow finch with streaking, the male Siskin has a smart black crown and a bib. In the breeding season the species is confined to areas with pine or spruce. At other times it is found in a wider variety of habitats, but particularly in areas with birch and alder, on which it feeds. It regularly attends bird feeders in winter. Siskins are not common residents, but many from northern and eastern Europe spend the winter in Britain from October to April.

 The sharply pointed bill is ideal for extracting the seeds of various trees, which provide the bulk of its diet.

 The nest is constructed from fir twigs lined with moss and hair, usually at a considerable height in a pine or spruce tree.

TRACK N° **56**

First the song, a rapid, undulating trilling, twittering and repeated call notes, plus a strangled, drawn-out nasal wheeze. Then some downwards inflected, clear *dju'ii* calls.

57 | Lesser Redpoll

This is a small, rather nondescript grey and brown finch, but capped with a splendid red fore-crown, or 'poll'. In spring the male also sports a pinkish-red throat and breast. Some individuals are resident, but many of our breeding birds apparently winter on the near Continent, while birds from further north move into Britain. Lesser Redpolls are generally distributed where there are extensive areas of birches, alders, willows and young conifers, but are nowhere common and have declined in recent decades.

 Seeds, especially those of birches, but insects are also taken when available.

 A small cup of grass and moss is built in a tree or bush.

TRACK N° **57**

First a series of long, rolling buzzing notes, *dzhiiirrrrr*, then slowly repeated *chechechecheche* calls.

58 | Linnet

For much of the year the Linnet is a plain brown and grey bird, but in spring the male develops an attractive grey head and a pinkish-red fore-crown and breast. The Linnet is found almost everywhere there is open ground with thick bushes, especially gorse and thorn. In winter it can also be found in fields, on rough and derelict ground, and in coastal marshes. It is sociable outside the breeding season, and is often seen in restless, constantly moving flocks. It favours bushy rural gardens and town gardens adjoining wasteground.

 Seeds of various plants, often weeds, but also insects when available.

 Builds a nest of fine twigs, grass and wool in a bush, especially gorse, or in thick ground cover.

TRACK N° 58

First the varied song of a male, a series of call-type notes interspersed with more musical whistles. Then the nasal staccato *chd'it chd'it* call.

59 | Yellowhammer

In summer the male Yellowhammer has a bright yellow head and breast; in winter the yellow is less evident, as in the female at all times. Otherwise the plumage is heavily streaked and chestnut-brown. Yellowhammers are mainly resident and widely distributed in open, bushy country, but have decreased alarmingly in recent decades, partly due to the reduction of hedgerows. Forming small flocks in winter and foraging around farmyards and stubble, often with sparrows and finches, they occur in rural gardens near mature hedgerows and forest edges.

 Seeds and grain, with insects in summer.

 Forms a nest of grass and moss on or near ground, on vegetated banks, in brambles or at hedgerow bottoms.

TRACK N° 59

The song, often quoted as a fast 'a little bit of bread' followed by a slow 'and no cheese'. Then the call, *djih*.

37

60 | Reed Bunting

In the breeding season the male is unmistakable, with a black head and throat, and a white moustache and neck collar, but in winter only vestiges of this distinctive plumage remain and he becomes a basically brown-above, white-below bird, streaked darker all over, like the female. Reed Buntings are resident and widely distributed wherever there are reed stands, marshes, bushy areas with damp ground, and gardens near to such habitats. In winter they are often found – along with other buntings and sparrows – around farmland, where food is easier to find.

 Mainly insects in summer, and seeds and grain in winter.

 Builds a nest of grass, reed blades and moss close to the ground in a tussock or low bush.

TRACK N° 60

Rapid song by unpaired male, then a slower halting, barely musical version with pauses between notes. Calls include a downwards inflected *tseeou* and a nasal rasping *djuh*.

OTHER BOOKS OF INTEREST

Barthel, Peter H. and Paschalis Dougalis, *New Holland European Bird Guide*, New Holland Publishers, 2008.

Bill Oddie's Introduction to Birdwatching, New Holland Publishers, 2002.

Burton, John A. and David Tipling, *Attracting Wildlife to Your Garden*, New Holland Publishers, 2006.

Golley, Mark, *Cooking for Birds*, New Holland Publishers, 2006.

Golley, Mark and Stephen Moss, *The Complete Garden Bird Book*, New Holland Publishers, 1996.

Oddie, Bill, *Garden Bird Year*, New Holland Publishers, 2009.

Whittley, Sarah, *The Garden Bird Book*, New Holland Publishers, 2007.

Young, Steve and Marianne Taylor, *Photographing Garden Wildlife*, New Holland Publishers, 2009.

SPECIES LIST

SPECIES LIST

	PAGE No	TRACK No		PAGE No	TRACK
Lesser Redpoll *Carduelis cabaret*	36	57	Rook *Corvus frugilegus*	32	48
Linnet *Carduelis cannabina*	37	58	Sedge Warbler *Acrocephalus schoenobaenus*	23	31
Long-tailed Tit *Aegithalos caudatus*	28	42	Siskin *Carduelis spinus*	36	56
Magpie *Pica pica*	30	45	Skylark *Alauda arvensis*	15	16
Mallard *Anas platyrhynchos*	7	1	Song Thrush *Turdus philomelos*	20	26
Marsh Tit *Parus palustris*	28	41	Sparrowhawk *Accipiter nisus*	9	4
Meadow Pipit *Anthus pratensis*	17	20	Starling *Sturnus vulgaris*	33	51
Mistle Thrush *Turdus viscivorus*	21	27	Stock Dove *Columba oenas*	12	9
Moorhen *Gallinula chloropus*	10	6	Swallow *Hirundo rustica*	16	18
Nuthatch *Sitta europaea*	29	43	Tawny Owl *Strix aluco*	14	13
Pheasant *Phasianus colchicus*	11	7	Treecreeper *Certhia familiaris*	30	44
Pied Wagtail *Motacilla alba yarrellii*	18	22	Willow Warbler *Phylloscopus trochilus*	25	36
Redwing *Turdus iliacus*	21	28	Woodpigeon *Columba palumbus*	13	11
Reed Bunting *Emberiza schoeniclus*	38	60	Wren *Troglodytes troglodytes*	19	23
Robin *Erithacus rubecula*	20	25	Yellowhammer *Emberiza citrinella*	37	59